30 Days of Forgiveness

Vandra Noel

Vandra Noel

Vandra Noel

Contents

Acknowledgement Page

Thank you to my counselor Ms. Soneakqua White for pulling some of the most hurtful events of my life out of me and teaching me how to live through it, let go of it and truly be free. There were many days my sessions were hard. The hurt and anger was choking the life out of me, but once I got there, she listened and heard me; she was attentive and spoke truth, so that I could experience peace.

Thank you to Dr. Regina Spellmon for not just being my pastor, but also my life coach. There were many times where I allowed people to pull me into their mess and the seed of anger and bitterness would fall and try to take root. Dr. Spellmon always said, "Don't allow anyone to pull you in their dysfunction, you just operate outside of it." I took her words to heart. Operating outside of others dysfunction helped me to do things with a clean heart and a right spirit.

Vandra Noel

I dedicate this book to all those who feel like forgiving others seems impossible and unfair!

Vandra Noel

Foreword

As I think about the title of this devotion, *30 Days of Forgiveness* I can't help but think about how difficult it was for me to forgive. I get a bit of anxiety just thinking about it. There have been so many episodes in my life that required forgiveness on my behalf. My thoughts were always, why should I forgive them when they hurt me. I didn't do anything. I'm sure you have felt that way as well. Once I understood forgiveness, it was never about what they did, it was about how I would choose to respond.

Forgiveness is a power that takes divine assistance to obtain. You can't forgive a deep hurt humanly without the Lord's reassurance that it's going to bring freedom in your life. You and I must forgive for God to forgive us. I had so many things that I just didn't want to let go of because I had a right not to forgive them. It's been said, that "unforgiveness is like drinking poison hoping the other person dies." That is such a true statement. Let it go so you can live!

There are so many misconceptions when it comes to forgiveness. I want to let you in on a few secrets that I learned from Bishop I.V. Hilliard years ago about forgiveness. First, forgiveness is not a feeling. You will never feel like it, so forgive and move on. Second, there is no such thing as forgive and forget. You don't have a sea of forgetfulness, only God does. You will remember the hurt, but over time it won't have the same impact to control you. And third, just because you forgive a person doesn't mean you have to bring them back into your life. My mom would always say, "feed them with a long handle spoon."

Forgiveness is a choice. Choosing to forgive gets your power back. You now are in control of your actions instead of the act controlling you. Remember it is a process. There will be triggers on the journey, but remember you have the power within to get through it.

30 Days of Forgiveness will be a great companion on your journey to forgiveness. If you're ready to walk in freedom and realign your life from the heartache you have experienced, then this book was designed just for you. I have had the opportunity to walk with Minister Vandra

Noel through many hurts and disappointments in her life. If anyone knows about forgiveness and what it takes to overcome the trauma of unforgiveness, she's the expert. Her devotional will accompany you in your process of forgiveness.

I can't wait to see what God is going to do through her life as she guides others through the triumphs and tragedies of her life. She is powerful, purposeful and loves people. I'm honored to call her Daughter. I love you to life!

Dr. Regina Spellmon

Vandra Noel

Dear Heavenly Father,

I come first of all giving you glory for the opportunity to unlock the doors of unforgiveness. Lord, I believe the person holding this book is ready to be free from all hurt, anger, shame, bitterness, and heaviness. I pray as they read each page, shackles will start falling, chains will begin to break and hearts will began to heal.

Thank You Lord for loving each of us enough to rescue us from ourselves and others. Thank You Jesus for paying the price on Calvary, but also for showing us that we have to forgive no matter what. Now bottle every tear Lord, hold our hands, and free our minds from overthinking and the torture that has bound us from happiness, peace, love, and truth. Thank You that after this book is read, the person reading it won't be the same. The fear that once existed will turn into freedom in Jesus Name! Now I plead the blood of Jesus Christ over everything concerning this person!

In Jesus Name,

Amen

Vandra Noel

And when you stand praying,
if you hold anything against anyone, forgive
them, so that your Father in
heaven may forgive you your sins.

Mark 11:25

Why Should I Forgive?

Many people walk around with a horrible disease that chips away at their life daily called unforgiveness. Unforgiveness is a very dark place to reside in. It is draining, life sapping and unhealthy. Unfortunately, there is no pill, drink or patch that can be used to cure it. Just like light can penetrate darkness to bring life to it, the only cure for unforgiveness is forgiveness. Let me ask you this... has unforgiveness attacked your life? If so, I have the recipe for the cure:

- Love
- Faith
- Confession
- Release
- Honesty
- Hope
- Jesus Christ

Together, these essential ingredients will

bring wholeness and healing to your mind, body, and soul.

I spent many days laying in my bed fat, unhappy, mad, sad, betrayed, overlooked, underappreciated, used, manipulated, mis-understood, lonely and downright tired! It was my fault I allowed other people's opinions, judgments, actions, deeds and thoughts of me to control me. I can't recall exactly how, when, where and why I gave people that much control over me? Nevertheless, I did and I desperately needed to give them over to God.

The people closest to me, hurt me the most because I gave them the power to come into my space and derail my life and emotions. It became common for me to have bitterness, unpleasant thoughts, and unkind words for them. I began to act and talk like the very person or persons that caused me harm and headache. I would always say, "I'm over it," but in reality, I was under it and it was sabotaging every aspect of my life. My health, relationships, marriage, and prayer life were on life support. I knew I needed God like never before. I needed to forgive. Not for them but to save me.

To be honest, what I was dealing with was depressing. Many times, we need to forgive the ones we deal with daily.

Forgiveness starts with an evaluation on ourselves first because you'll need to identify the things within you that needs to be corrected. This will prevent you from walking in circles repeating the same acts that hurt you in the first place with different people.

Forgiveness is not a feeling, but a fact that when we forgive, we are forgiven. Humanity and flesh together equals frailty, flaws, and fear. Just the slightest action or deed done to us by someone that offends us will cause us to have anger, malice, and unforgiveness. It's all a trick of the enemy to keep God's children in bondage.

When we try to rationalize with God, we immediately miss the mark. Pleading our case, even though it may be a great case, it doesn't mean God will side with us. God doesn't think like us. His thoughts and ways are much higher. Thinking that a big God will stoop to our level and be okay with our temper tantrums is hideous.

No, we must rise up over every hurt, betrayal, lie, and misfortune that others do to us or that we do to ourselves because Jesus was lifted up to draw us to Him. So many times we think we've forgiven someone, but when we see them, hear their name or think about them and something in us feels uneasy or a rage, we are still in bondage.

Sitting back one day thinking about how God has allowed people to hurt me, mistreat me, abandon me, and walk all over me and He not do anything. The anger settled deeper in my mind more and more while I asked God, "Do you see me? Have you heard them? Why haven't you dealt with them?" Immediately God says, "My grace and mercy work for them as it works for you. I'm long-suffering and patient with them, just as I am with you."

God asked,

"Do you really want me to get them, punish them and deal with them right now?"

I said, "Yes Lord!"

He said, "Ok, well let me start with your unforgiving self. Let me punish you, get you and deal with you first!"

Stopping in my tracks, I saw skid marks. I didn't want it to be about what I've done. In my mind, I am the victim not the bad guy. My thoughts, my heart, my words, and my deeds spelled out hypocrite and unfor-giveness. Many times we see and feel what others do to us, but standing on the other side of the spectrum, we fail to see or feel what we spew out to others. I don't care how good we think we are, we are a mess. So before we pull out our 'woe is me' cards, let's remember the cards we passed out.

Forgive so that we can be forgiven. How do we think we got in with Christ? The blood washes our sins away and Christ forgives us. Forgiveness is not giving people who hurt us keys to re-enter our life. Forgiveness is freeing ourselves from bitterness and opening the path for God to forgive us. When people show us who they are, we should believe them and we should also forgive them. It is true, hurt people hurt people; angry people are dangerous people; sneaky people can't be trusted people.

Think about it, how many times does God forgive us in one day? How many times in a day do we disappoint, disrespect and destroy our witness before God? Yet in turn, we fold our arms, work our neck and harden our heart to those who disappoint, disrespect and destroy our name.

We have to learn to forgive and move on. Not forgiving is not moving on, it's standing still and being stuck right in that place where the hurt started. It's not healthy nor beneficial to hold on to hurt. We will never feel like forgiving someone, but it's a must, especially if we plan on moving on with our lives. Forgiveness and freedom are real and necessary.

The next step to helping yourself forgive is admitting that you are hurt and angry. Admit to yourself and others that you've been abused, misused, rejected, and mishandled. Get emotionally and mentally undressed before God. He knows all of your complaints, but now He wants to hear it come out of your mouth. The more we express it, the more we release it. Holding it is holding us back. Keeping it is keeping us in bondage. Reliving it is remaining in the hurt. Forgiving is not forgetting, its moving forward.

Unforgiveness makes the person you're holding a grudge against more important than they actually are. Forgiving them and moving on makes them irrelevant. Forgiving yourself removes you out the box so you could grow, whereas not forgiving yourself locks you in a space that hinders your growth.

Freedom is just that…freeing you from the dumb stuff. It's as simple as that. You don't have to forgive them personally, but you must forgive them emotionally to move on. We also must ask for forgiveness whether they accept our apologies or not. We have to be free to move on.

Lastly, the hardest person to ask for forgiveness is ourselves. But, if we don't move past the pain, we will be bound and blame the world for our own self-inflicted wounds! Admit you're wrong and ask God to forgive you. We have to move forward and see what's on the other side of forgiveness. We deserve it.

Vandra Noel

Day 1

I sought the LORD, and he answered me; he
delivered me from all my fears.

Psalms 34:4

We Can't Fix What We Refuse to Face!

First and foremost I need you to understand that you can't keep hiding your hurts. Masking it will never make the pain you feel from it go away. So many times I've refused to express how I felt because most of the time, the person that hurt me, turned the blame on me. To avoid further problems, I suppressed my hurt or took the blame to try and salvage the relationship.

It's okay to say, "I've been hurt, used and mistreated." It's ok to say, "Something is wrong!" Acting like your feelings aren't valid, only intensifies the pain. Admit that you have pain and then acknowledge who caused it. If we don't take this step, we can't move forward.

Scripture Reference:

Psalms 34:8
Proverbs 18:10

Reflections

Psalms 51:10

1. Write down the types of situations where you tend to suppress your thoughts or feelings.

_____

_____

_____

_____

2. What thoughts or feelings do you suppress?

_____

_____

_____

_____

3. Write or say how you truly feel during those situations?

_____

_____

_____

_____

Day 2

Casting all your care upon him;
for he careth for you.

---

1 Peter 5:7

Let Go and Let God

Let it go! No one holds us back more than ourselves. I know you're probably saying, "You don't know what happened to me, it's not that easy to let it go! You don't know what they did, said, how they treated me, left me, abused me, discredited me, used me, how many times they cheated on me, stole from me, or how they robbed me of my peace." Or you may be thinking, "You don't know the bad choices I made. My life is messed up and I can't move forward. I can't forgive myself and I will never be happy again."

You're absolutely right, I don't know, but God does. He is waiting for you to tell Him all about it. He wants you to take it out of your heart and hands to give it all to Him. He will never judge or forsake you, but He will love you and show you how to love yourself and others again.

Believe it or not, it takes more energy and causes more pain to our relationships and mind to hold onto hurt, bad choices, guilt, worry, losses, slander, and of course unforgiveness. It's like carrying a backpack full of huge heavy rocks all day every day.

Take the pressure off yourself, your heart, mind, and body by taking that backpack off and laying it at the feet of Jesus. We have to be true to ourselves. Every time you think about it, let it go. Even if it has to be done every hour, every day, every month, or every minute, release and let it all go!

Forgiveness is the door to healing, confidence, deliverance, blessings, peace, hope, living and freedom. The key is called release. By releasing it you are taking the first steps towards freeing yourself from unnecessary burdens and heartache that can potentially stay with you for years to come.

Scripture Reference:

Psalm 46:10
Isaiah 43:18

Reflections

Ephesians 4:31-32

Journal your feelings and your pain. This is a great way to start your release. If we don't do this, we can't move forward.

1. Write down a few of the experiences that you feel have held you back.

_____

_____

_____

_____

_____

2. What are a few of the bad decisions you believe hold you back from moving forward?

_____

_____

_____

_____

_____

_____

Day 3

Be sober, be vigilant; because your adversary
the devil, as a roaring lion, walketh about,
seeking whom he may devour:

---

1 Peter 5:8

Don't Over Think It!

When we make up our minds to forgive,
the enemy starts to taunt and tell us we are
crazy. Overthinking and trying to rationalize
and make sense of it all, will keep you in a
mental tug of war. Remember, the enemy's
plan is to devour us and destroy us.

The enemy will literally talk you into
picking up what you let go of because he
believes in "Bondage over Freedom".

Say to yourself until it's playing in your
mind like a broken record, "The devil is a
liar! The devil is a liar! The devil is a liar!"

Scripture Reference:

Exodus 14:14
Proverbs 4:23

Reflections

1. Did you feel the unforgiveness try to rise up again?

_____

_____

_____

_____

2. What are the thoughts that recycle in your mind?

_____

_____

_____

_____

3. What can you say to offset the negative thoughts that replay in your mind and encourage yourself?

_____

_____

_____

_____

Day 4

Take heed to yourselves: If thy brother
trespass against thee, rebuke him; and if he
repent, forgive him.

And if he trespass against thee seven times in
a day, and seven times in a day turn again to
thee, saying, I repent; thou shalt forgive him.

Luke 17:3-4

They Keep Hurting Me!

I know when I started walking in
forgiveness, it seemed like the ones who hurt
me before hurt me again, lied to me again,
abused me again and I messed up again.

What am I supposed to do? This
forgiveness walk isn't working. I keep
making the same decisions that always leave
me hurt and disappointed. I keep allowing
the same people to keep getting away with
the same things.

You may not want to hear this, but we
have to forgive over and over again, even if
it's the same offense in the same day. It made
me angry thinking about it and I wanted to
debate it with the Lord. However, what God
said broke me down. He said, "I forgive you

many times in a day for the same things. I keep forgiving you because I am love and I want you to experience my love, so that you will know how to exhibit love."

Scripture Reference:

Isaiah 1:18
Matthew 6:14-15

Reflections

1. Write your thoughts about Day 4. How do you feel today?

_____

_____

_____

_____

2. What types of things did you need to forgive today?

_____

_____

_____

_____

3. How many times did you have to forgive today?

_____

_____

_____

_____

Day 5

For if ye forgive men their trespasses, your heavenly Father will also forgive you:

But if ye forgive not men their trespasses, neither will your Father forgive your trespasses.

Mark 11:25

When I Move, He moves JUST LIKE THAT...

The title is the only part of a song's lyrics that I can remember...it's my version of the song anyway. It's been said that when we make one step, God will make the next. It's the same concept with forgiveness. How long will God have to wait on us to move? He is not waiting on us for His own sake, but He is waiting on us for ours. We can't ask for or expect to receive what we refuse to give.

Scripture Reference:

1 John 1:9
Ephesians 4:31-32

Reflections

Think about the people, times in your life and things you need to forgive. Remember, for everything you forgive and release, God is released to forgive you as well.

1. What do you need God to forgive you for?

_____

_____

_____

_____

2. List the people in your life you need to forgive?

_____

_____

_____

_____

3. What situations or people do you need to release and move on from?

_____

_____

_____

_____

Day 6

And when ye stand praying, forgive, if ye have ought against any: that your Father also which is in heaven may forgive you your trespasses.

Mark 11:25

A Hard Heart

As I sat at a red light one day, I'd only sat there for a little over a minute and already I felt my patience running out quickly. The lanes next to me as well as the cars on the other opposite side of the street were zipping by freely, no obstacles or hindrances.

I was listening to a praise and worship song and the lyrics were, *God's tryna tell ya something, tell me can you hear Him* and it repeated the chorus again. I looked up and the light was still red and now I'm fuming. I think to myself , *God is not trying to tell something, knowing I'm trying to get to work...*

All of sudden I hear God say, "Everyone around you is moving but you, because you're still holding on to unforgiveness!"

Really God? I told God that I did forgive. He

said, "Your mouth said it, but your heart didn't mean it. Until you turn your heart to me, you won't be able to move on with your life. Ask me to help you and I will." I asked for help with tears in my eyes and at that moment the light turned green.

Scripture Reference:

Psalm 51:10
Ezekiel 11:19

Reflections

Are you stuck because your heart isn't right? Only you can change it by asking God for help. Write down your thoughts.

1. Do you feel as if you're stuck in some areas of your life? What are they?

_____

_____

_____

_____

2. Evaluate your heart. List the times you said that you've forgiven, but didn't mean it.

_____

_____

_____

_____

Day 7

Judge not, and ye shall not be judged:
condemn not, and ye shall not be condemned:
forgive, and ye shall be forgiven:

Luke 6:37

Those Caught and Those Covered

There are two categories of human beings; those that are caught in their sins and those who are covered by God's grace and mercy. One time, I was so furious with a family member because of how they behaved. I pointed out their faults and shortcomings that seemed ridiculous to me. I was immediately convicted for judging and condemning them for their choices. Just because no one knew about my sin and foolishness didn't mean I hadn't done what I condemned them for.

God said, "Ok, let's even the score. I'll take grace, mercy, and forgiveness off the table since you're having such a hard time doing things my way."

Right now I want you to do a strong evaluation of yourself. Are you a judgmental person? Are you passing judgement on an act you have been delivered from or once thought about doing yourself? We all sin and fall short of the glory of God. Therefore, we have no room to look down on someone just because we don't like their behaviors. The only way to forgive for real is to uncover yourself before a loving caring God. Take your eyes off them and put them on your relationship with God. Pray for them and keep going.

Scripture Reference:

James 5:9
Ephesians 4:32

Reflections

1. Have you been guilty of judging someone for something you did in the past but are now delivered from?

_____

_____

_____

_____

2. What made you change or what caused you to change?

_____

_____

_____

_____

3. Write a prayer for the deliverance of the one or ones your judging. Remember God answers prayers.

_____

_____

_____

_____

Day 8

Dearly beloved, avenge not yourselves, but rather give place unto wrath: for it is written, Vengeance is mine; I will repay, saith the Lord.

Romans 12:19

Fueling Your Feelings

Get it out of your mind about hurting people in the same way they hurt you. No, it's not fair, but taking revenge is not paying someone back. It's opening yourself up to be just like them. It's not worth it! Fueling your feelings with bitterness, rage, anger, and harm is unhealthy, destroys your peace and hurts your credibility and integrity. You have to release those that hurt you to God.

It is His responsibility to decide what justice looks like and to watch over you. It is your responsibility to cast all your cares upon Him, so He can love, heal and pour into all of you. Forgiveness cannot take place until you surrender all your hurt, anger and plots to pay them back. Trust God to be the Judge and the Healer you need.

Vandra Noel

Scripture Reference:

Leviticus 19:18
Isiah 54:17

Reflections

1. What does surrender look like to you?

_____

_____

_____

_____

2. Are you really ready to surrender?

_____

_____

_____

_____

3. Journal a prayer of surrender and trust
God to help you.

_____

_____

_____

_____

_____

_____

_____

Day 9

Keep thy heart with all diligence;
for out of it are the issues of life.

Proverbs 4:23

Heart Check

Many of us pay close attention to what we eat and other things we put in our body to stay healthy. But, what about what we allow into our Spirit? What we consume and participate in takes up residence in our heart. Think on this...is your heart filled with malice, anger, and unforgiveness? If so, you have true heart disease. Understand that what you consume, also pours out. Be sure to get your fill of real love, forgiveness, peace, and hope. So that you can continue to speak life and positivity to those you come in contact with. Check your heart today!

Scripture Reference:

Proverbs 13:3
Luke 6:45

Reflections

Take a moment to write your feelings so that you can see the condition of your heart.

1. If you need a little work, what things can you do each day to have a healthier heart?

_____

_____

_____

_____

_____

_____

_____

_____

_____

_____

_____

_____

_____

_____

_____

_____

_____

Day 10

So when they continued asking him, he lifted up himself, and said unto them, He that is without sin among you, let him first cast a stone at her.

John 8:7

Expecting Perfection

Do you believe you are you perfect? Have you done everything right? Are you the perfect one in the family, on your job, out of all your friends and at your church?

Of course not, so why do we expect that from others? Sin means to miss the mark. In Romans 3:23 it says, *"For all have sinned, and come short of the glory of God."* The word 'all' is what stands out in that passage. So because we are not perfect creatures, we 'all' are often guilty ourselves of missing the mark.

We have to re-think the we way handle the people who have hurt us by looking at ourselves first. We can be so hard on the people who hurt us. Why? Did they do something worse than we ever have? If the shoe were on the other foot, would it be okay for someone to hold you to the same standards or expectations that you have for others? How would you feel if someone treated you with the same measure of anger or disgust that you do them?

We all sometimes feel justified in how we feel, but does that mean we can measure the depths of sin for each other? If you're so perfect, holy, and sanctified, gather your stones and throw all of them at your oppressors. Chances are you'd catch a few stones in the process. Instead of taking your judgements out on others, it's better to cry, scream, kick or do whatever you have to, to get through what you feel because none of us are prepared to cast the first stone. Trust God to be our perfect God. It's so much better to forgive and praise God that He hasn't stoned us yet.

Scripture Reference:

Colossians 4;6
Matthew 7:1-5

Reflections

1. Think of the people you've judged because they didn't meet your expectations. What judgements would they have of you?

_____

_____

_____

_____

2. Take a moment to pray and forgive them. Journal your thoughts.

_____

_____

_____

_____

_____

_____

_____

_____

_____

_____

_____

Day 11

Blessed are the pure in heart:
for they shall see God.

Matthew 5:8

Do We Want to See God?

Heaven and Hell is real and quite possible our destination in the afterlife. Imagine seeing rude, cursing, mean and contentious people walking the streets of gold. It's contrary to everything we've learned to believe.

I remember trying to get into a gated community to see a friend. The guard at the gate asked for a lot of information and identification before he let me through the gates. They didn't allow just anyone in their community. So why should God allow just anyone to enter the pearly gates of His heavenly community, especially with an unclean heart, full of anger and unforgiveness?

Scripture Reference:

Psalm 24:4
Hebrews 12:14

Reflections

Write what would cause you not to enter God's community and what you could work on to eliminate them from your life.

_____

_____

_____

_____

_____

_____

_____

_____

_____

_____

_____

_____

_____

_____

_____

_____

Day 12

> The thief cometh not, but for to steal,
> and to kill, and to destroy: I am come
> that they might have life, and that
> they might have it more abundantly.

John 10:10

An Unfair Crime

Would you invite a thief into your home? Would you allow a killer to take the life of your husband, wife, child or friend? Would you befriend someone who destroyed your property?

If you answered 'No' to all of these questions, then why do you act as an accessory to all the above?

The enemy wants to steal our peace, kill our hope and destroy our reputation and relationship with others. When we don't forgive we become accessory to all he has plotted to do.

He wants you to be focused on who you're mad at so he can create more division and disruption between you; taking your eyes off God and further away from your purpose. The enemy will create an issue and use you to be the getaway driver, leave you to hold the bag of hatred and unforgiveness in your heart and then say he didn't tell you to do it. He knows that united in Christ, we are powerful. He cannot deter us off our path or cause us to forget whom we belong to. He also doesn't have the access or ability to drain us of our power, purpose, or authority. We have God, the Word and each other to guard against the wiles of the enemy. Don't get locked up in a mental and emotional cell of unforgiveness. It will rob you of peace and God's blessings...and that would truly be a crime.

Scripture Reference:

John 10:1
John 6:33

Reflections

Think on the people you felt robbed you of the things you had or loved (peace, joy, blessings, etc.). Write their name and list what they took from you next to it.

1. You may need additional notebook paper to complete this exercise.

---

2. When looking back on any of those situations, past or current, is there a possibility of reconciliation or forgiveness? If yes, what could you do to initiate it?

_____

_____

_____

_____

_____

_____

_____

_____

_____

_____

_____

_____

_____

_____

_____

_____

_____

Take a moment to pray for and forgive each person. Then reclaim those things taken, trusting and believing that they are yours, in Jesus name.

Day 13

If ye shall ask any thing in my name,
I will do it.

John 14:14

Asking for Help

I remember as if it were yesterday that I asked God to help me to forgive someone in my family. I was totally honest with God about how I felt, how I hurt and even how I didn't care if I ever saw that person again. But then, I felt overwhelming sadness because that's not how I wanted to feel. However, in that moment it was the only option in my mind. I asked God to help me forgive them for my sake and for Him to get all the Glory. I needed relief from my own guilt. I remember saying,

> *"Lord, you're my Heavenly Father and if I can't trust anyone to help me, I know you will. Heal my heart and clear my mind not for me to forget, but for me to forgive. It's a choice and I'm making a choice to ask for help that is beyond me."*

Many of us don't know how to forgive for real. Stop asking mama, daddy and them for permission and what they think. They are flesh just like you. Ask Your Father in Heaven who is a master at forgiving.

Scripture Reference:

Psalms 46: 1-3
Philippians 4: 6-7

Reflections

---

1. Ask God for help in your own way.
Journal your thoughts.

_____

_____

_____

_____

_____

_____

_____

_____

_____

_____

_____

_____

_____

_____

_____

_____

_____

Day 14

Wherefore seeing we also are compassed about with so great a cloud of witnesses, let us lay aside every weight, and the sin which doth so easily beset us, and let us run with patience the race that is set before us.

Hebrews 12:1

The Load

It's so easy to get entangled, engulfed and engaged in things that literally sap our energy. Life situations, death, divorce, separation, rejection, abandonment, fear, loss, and even self-hate weigh in on us, causing us to feel like giving up. Instead of surrendering all these real issues to God, we hold onto them and adopt them into our everyday life. Eventually, they leave us numb and detached from everyone and everything.

Our daily journey is not as easy as it could be, should be, or ought to be because we've allowed unforgiveness to take root and latch on. It's time for you to unload all the things weighing you down. Drop it all and pick up the faith you need to see what's on the other side of forgiveness.

Scripture Reference:

Luke 21:34
2 Timothy 4:7

Reflections

1. What's in your emotional backpack? Write down the things that weigh you down.

_____

_____

_____

_____

_____

_____

_____

2. Write down situations from the past that weigh you down?

_____

_____

_____

_____

_____

_____

_____

_____

Day 15

Now I beseech you, brethren, mark them
which cause divisions and offences contrary
to the doctrine which ye have learned;
and avoid them.

For they that are such serve not our Lord
Jesus Christ, but their own belly; and by
good words and fair speeches deceive
the hearts of the simple.

Romans 16:17-18

The Ego Syndrome

Do you know anyone who has held
things over someone else's head forever?
Every time a conversation arises this person
tries to manipulate, mishandle and even
misconstrue events. Their vile intent flows
out of their mouth like venom. They mean to
keep their victim hostage to their anger.

The power of control washes over them
as they crush the spirit of the person before
them. Their ego requires constant attention
or else risk being deflated. They feed it by
depleting others of joy and freedom. This
person is dangerous and has no sign of God
in them. In truth, they are powerless people

with a hidden agenda to keep the person they are angry with locked up in emotional shame and guilt. These types of people you must separate yourself from, forgive and give them to God. Don't give them control of you any longer.

Scripture Reference:

Jude 1:19
2 Timothy 3:5

Reflections

Those who hold the past over you are stuck in the past themselves. They are in bondage to the anger they feel and are unable to free themselves from it. While they are unable to get unstuck, they can attempt to drag you down. Misery does love company. That is why it is important to create distance between you and find it in your heart to forgive them. They hurt deeply and need God too, but they don't need to hurt you in the process. Take time to pray and journal your thoughts.

_____

_____

_____

_____

_____

_____

_____

_____

_____

_____

Day 16

For God's will was for us to be
made holy by the sacrifice of the body
of Jesus Christ, once for all time.

Hebrews 10:10

Shame is a Set-Up

All of us have made some unfavorable choices. We look back on them and cringe. God knows all we've done and all we will do. For that reason He sent Jesus to earth to live, shed blood, die, rise and intercede on our behalf. I don't care what you've done, the blood of Jesus cleanses and saves. All you have to do ask for forgiveness.

Forgive yourself! I speak shame off of you. I speak depression off of you. I speak giving up off of you. In its place, I speak freedom, life, hope, joy, love and salvation!

Forgive YOU!

Scripture Reference:

Romans 6:6
2 Thessalonians 2:13

Reflections

What do you want to replace shame with…truth, love, freedom? Think about it and journal your thoughts.

_____

_____

_____

_____

_____

_____

_____

_____

_____

_____

_____

_____

_____

_____

_____

_____

Day 17

Charity suffereth long, and is kind;
charity envieth not; charity vaunteth
not itself, is not puffed up,

Doth not behave itself unseemly,
seeketh not her own, is not
easily provoked, thinketh no evil;

Rejoiceth not in iniquity, but
rejoiceth in the truth;

Beareth all things, believeth all things,
hopeth all things, endureth all things.

---

1 Corinthians 13:4-7

Their Life, Your Unforgiveness

Many of us are angry and holding
unforgiveness in our hearts because of
decisions other people have made with their
life. You're locked in a cell of anger with no
bars because you expected more of them,
from them, and out of them. The root of it all
is disappointment. Let go of the expectations
you had of them. We are not God, we don't
know what path God has set for them or us.
Stay in your lane and forgive them.

Truth be told they don't need our comments, condemnation, or criticism, because they are already having a hard time forgiving themselves. They need forgiveness, encouragement, and maybe even support. God knows His children's plans, but not us. Pray God's healing, deliverance, and peace over their life.

Scripture Reference:

1 John 4:11
1 Peter 4:8
Jeremiah 29:11

Reflections

What decisions in life have you made that may have disappointed someone or even yourself? Pray about it, write and release it.

_____

_____

_____

_____

_____

_____

_____

_____

_____

_____

_____

_____

_____

_____

_____

_____

_____

Day 18

For I know the thoughts that I think toward you, saith the Lord, thoughts of peace, and not of evil, to give you an expected end.

Then shall ye call upon me, and ye shall go and pray unto me, and I will hearken unto you.

And ye shall seek me, and find me, when ye shall search for me with all your heart.

Jeremiah 29:11-13

God's Plan

Have you ever been furious with someone you thought had your back? Well I have. When I was a caregiver, I felt all alone. All of the people who promised to help only did so when they wanted to and not when I needed them. I began to harbor feelings of anger and resentment. It consumed me. Seeds of unforgiveness deposited in my heart because of the excuses I heard.

One day God said, "This assignment is yours. I'll send the help you need, but when I don't, know I'm there with you. Get your mind off of what they aren't doing and focus your mind on me. This is all a part of the plan I have for YOU, not them. Let It Go!"

Scripture Reference:

Micah 4:12
Job 23:13

Reflections

1. Describe the situations where you needed help, but didn't receive it.

_____

_____

_____

_____

_____

_____

2. Sometimes the plan God has for you does not include the presence or help of others. Understanding this, how does it change your perspective or heart regarding those situations?

_____

_____

_____

_____

_____

_____

_____

Day 19

Not to all the people, but unto
witnesses chosen before God, even
to us, who did eat and drink with him
after he rose from the dead.

Acts 10:41

Still Here!

Do you know no one can stop, hinder or cancel out God's blessings on your life? Sometimes it's the people closest to you who will hurt your feelings, be jealous of you and the anointing on your life and try to kill your dreams. It's none of your business what they think or say. They don't run anything and they certainly can't stop you, God's child!

In the midst of their plots, don't you dare become distracted, discouraged and do not allow anger to fester in your heart for them. Release them and give your mind and heart space away from the negativity.

Unforgiveness is a sneaky emotion that'll creep up on you, move in, get comfortable, and become a resident in your heart. Just because you've separated yourself from the people who hurt you, doesn't mean the painful emotions left. If you don't acknowledge your pain and forgive, bitterness can seep into your healthy relationships and daily interactions. You too could be guilty of hurting someone as a result. Pray and give your sorrows to God. Let Him address those who've come against you. God's plan in the end is to raise you up, if you don't give up. They tried it and God turned it. You keep your head high and your seat full at God's table. You're still here!

Scripture Reference:

Genesis 45:1:8
Isaiah 42:14

Reflections

The best way to see God move in your life, is to recount how you have progressed or moved on since being betrayed from someone closest to you. Journal what you've done and/or accomplished since that time.

Day 20

Bless those who persecute you;
bless and do not curse.

Romans 12:14

Pray for Who?

The hardest thing God has ever told me to do was pray for my enemies. I read that scripture over and over again because clearly God didn't mean that. Oh, I had prayers for them alright! It went like this:

Lord,

Get them, hurt them, make them feel the hurt they rendered to me!

But that's not God. He's not the boogie man who goes after those you try to sick Him on. He's a loving God who is trying to draw our accusers unto Him by extending grace, just like He did for us when we were guilty of wrongdoing.

When you feel like you can't pray for them remember someone prayed for you after you hurt, betrayed, lied on, and abused them. Every now and then we have to remember that we've preyed on others and needed prayer.

Scripture Reference:

1Peter 3:9
Romans 12:17

Reflections

Exercise: Pray for someone who has really hurt you. Matthew 5:44

Write down your thoughts.

_____

_____

_____

_____

_____

_____

_____

_____

_____

_____

_____

_____

_____

_____

_____

_____

Day 21

While we look not at the things which are seen, but at the things which are not seen: for the things which are seen are temporal; but the things which are not seen are eternal.

2 Corinthians 4:18

Focus

So how are you doing with this 'Let it go' forgiveness thing? Changing our focus helps us to move forward and not be stuck on pain.

Anyone who knows me knows that I'm terrified of bugs; from the tiniest to the largest. I remember being paralyzed in fear watching a bug crawling on the wall. I needed to know his next move, because it would help determine mine. My husband would always say, "Girl that bug is not thinking about you and you sitting over here looking crazy. Kill that bug so you can go and do what you have to do!"

Like in dealing with the bug, when I focus on those who hurt me I become paralyzed by the pain instead of killing it in my heart. Nine times out of ten those we are refusing to forgive aren't even thinking about us. They sleep well at night and have moved on with their life while we are stuck in anger and missing out on our life!

Re-aligning our focus to God and following Him creates distance between that thing that paralyzed us and gives us the grace to heal. One day you'll look around and what once paralyzed and hurt, or mini-mized us is no longer there; only proof of abundance, blessings and a life well lived. Keep your focus on God.

Scripture Reference:

Romans 8:24-25
Hebrews 11:1

Reflections

1. What and who has you paralyzed?

_____

_____

_____

_____

_____

2. What types of distractions cause your focus to stray from God?

_____

_____

_____

_____

_____

3. Journal your thoughts about situations that you've overcome by changing your focus.

_____

_____

_____

_____

_____

Day 22

Judge not, and ye shall not be judged: condemn
not, and ye shall not be condemned: forgive,
and ye shall be forgiven:

Luke 6:37

Safe From the Storm

Whether we want to admit it or not
Satan is the root of all evil, especially in the
buildings where we gather in to fellowship.
Church hurt is real and it happens more
often than not. But if we are to be 'The
Church', then we must recognize that like
buildings, not all people are stable, reliable or
able to protect. Because of these experiences,
we use a broad brush to typecast all churches
as evil or flawed. Realistically, when one
building is condemned or burned down,
does it imply that all other buildings are
unsafe as well? A common outcome is we
magnify an issue that drives us to stay away
from 'The Church' or the place where unity
provides strength, support and protection
from where the storms of life can destroy us.

Noah was instructed to build an ark for
his family and animals. Can you imagine
being confined on an ark for 40 days and 40

nights straight? Not only was space limited, but they had to endure the smell and mess with no relief. They couldn't get mad and get off the Ark, because God sent an intense downpour of rain to kill every living thing. In spite of the conditions on the Ark, God equipped them to get along with each other.

So you're telling me, we can't stay a couple of hours in a building with each other? We focus too much on the mess instead of the *Message* that can help us with the mess and messy people. The point is, don't let anyone ever make you jump ship. Going back out into the world after God has led us to the protection of fellowship with each other, leaves us to be subject to the unknown dangers. Forgive and stay free in fellowship.

I'm not by any means condoning hurt from church folks. They are flawed and fickle human beings just like we are. What I am promoting is to stay close to the Father, stay on the Ark and watch God work it all out. God knows those who hurt us and He will make it right.

Scripture Reference:

Genesis 7: 1-9
James 4: 11-12

Reflections

Have you been hurt by church folks? Don't miss your blessing by focusing on the mess. Tell God all about it and He will make it all right. Journal your thoughts.

_____

_____

_____

_____

_____

_____

_____

_____

_____

_____

_____

_____

_____

_____

_____

_____

Day 23

Casting all your care upon him;
for he careth for you.

---

1 Peter 5:7

Who Am I?

I greatly dislike having junk all around me. Unclean rooms and the sight of things thrown about takes me out! I realize that clean surroundings and things in order keep my thinking clean and in order. All things don't need to be kept. Some things need to be let go to make room for new or better, should you want it. It's the same concept for the memories we're attached to. We stay stagnant and cluttered with shame, guilt, depression, anger and it doesn't leave room for us to receive God's blessings. They need to be released or it can literally take you down.

But what about unforgiveness? I stewed over how I was hurt, mistreated and talked about. I replayed in my mind how they walked off, took things from me and moved on with their life. It was as if I never existed and I lost so much trying to keep them and make them happy. I felt abused and I... I didn't realize I was an emotional and mental hoarder! I kept piling on all things people did to me in my spirit, my heart and on my mind instead of releasing it. Why did I hold on to it? Why did I replay what happened in my head where it's always in the forefront of my mind? Replaying it controlled my thoughts and emotions. No wonder I was worn out! It took so much from me that I wasn't present in my daily life. I wasn't who God purposed me to be...I was a shell. I was trapped in my own misery. Unforgiveness took my mind and my identity.

Scripture Reference:

Ecclesiastes 3:6
Ephesians 4:31-32

Reflections

1. Are you an emotional hoarder? Start to decluttering by writing in your journal those things you replay in your mind.

_____

_____

_____

_____

_____

_____

_____

_____

_____

_____

_____

_____

_____

_____

_____

_____

2. Pray and release those emotions to God. Forgive those who hurt you and forgive yourself. Let it go and make room for more. Journal your thoughts and feelings at this moment.

_____

_____

_____

_____

_____

_____

_____

_____

_____

_____

_____

_____

_____

_____

_____

_____

_____

_____

Day 24

Keeping mercy for thousands, forgiving
iniquity and transgression and sin, and that
will by no means clear the guilty; visiting the
iniquity of the fathers upon the children, and
upon the children's children, unto the third
and to the fourth generation.

Exodus 34:7

Generational Curses

There are so many generational curses
passed down in our families it sickens me.
Some curses are so obvious that even a blind
man can see it. Curses such as adultery,
unwed child birth, alcoholism, drug
addictions, incarceration, gang affiliation,
and promiscuous life styles. I'm not
condoning any of these curses, however the
biggest one that is never mentioned nor
addressed is manipulation and
unforgiveness.

This horrible stench of dysfunction is
passed down through the generations and
we wonder why families don't stick together,
don't love, don't forgive and don't live in
harmony. When children see their parents,

gossiping, bickering and holding grudges with other family members the seed is replanted and is destined to take root.

If we don't teach truth, integrity or forgiveness and live accordingly in our actions, we will see in the generations to come those same unfavorable behaviors. They watch and mimic everything we do even down to our unforgiveness. Let's break our generational curses by living in Christ.

Scripture Reference:

Exodus 20:5-6
Deuteronomy 5:9-10

Reflections

BREAK THE CURSE!!!
ASK GOD TO SEVERE IT AT THE ROOT!!!

Break the generational curse of manipulation
and unforgiveness by asking God to sever it
at the root. Pray and journal your thoughts.

_____

_____

_____

_____

_____

_____

_____

_____

_____

_____

_____

_____

_____

_____

_____

Day 25

If the Son therefore shall make you free,
ye shall be free indeed.

John 8:36

Free Means Free

I will never forget the time I asked God to free me from a relationship that totally destroyed me emotionally and mentally. I kept asking for a way out and vowed if the Lord let me out I would not turn back. But I lied. I kept going back to the same place God freed me from because it was familiar. Those familiar feelings, failures and fears instantly locked me back into anger for that person. As deeply as it hurt me, I was more afraid of the unknown than I was of the pain I knew I was going to experience.

God said so plainly one day, *"I set you free. You are the one putting yourself back in their emotional prison of pain!"*

Forgiveness is not easy. It becomes harder to do when you allow that same person to hurt you again. You know that you put yourself back in the place God set you free from. There is shame and guilt attached to knowing you did this to yourself.

Forgiveness does not mean forgiving the person who hurt you and then placing them back on the front row seats of your life. Give yourself space and time to heal and forgive for real. Forgive yourself and show yourself the same devotion and attention you gave to those who were so undeserving. God frees you so that someone worthy can and occupy those seats to your life. More importantly, so that you can fully realize how loved and valuable you are. All others can be forgiven and loved from afar. When The Son of God sets us free from some people, we need to stay free!

Scripture Reference:

Galatians 5:1
Luke 4:18

Reflections

1. Who has God freed you from that you repeatedly let back in?

_____

_____

_____

_____

2. What are those familiar things that make you feel safe to return that person?

_____

_____

_____

_____

3. Pray freedom for that person and yourself? Journal your thoughts.

_____

_____

_____

_____

_____

_____

Day 26

The Lord is gracious, and full of compassion;
slow to anger, and of great mercy.

Psalm 145:8

Torturing Ourselves to DEATH

Unforgiveness is a torture that only we can control. It is a chronic anger classified in medical books as a disease and has been linked to heart disease, diabetes, cancers, high blood pressure and immune diseases. Studies show 61% of cancer patients have cancer because of unforgiveness. Now what we eat and don't eat may contribute to our health, however you can be fit, fine and full of unforgiveness. It will eventually lead to health issues.

Negative emotions, anger, and hatred creates chronic anxiety. Many doctors now are healing patients by walking them through the process of forgiveness. So many of us are holding on to childhood hurt and find our later days are filled with sickness, regret and torture. How dare we hold on to unforgiveness for years at a time when God forgives us daily. Check your heart and identify those people, places or things that torture and are slowly killing your health and quality of life.

If you are sick check your heart and what's in it. If it's unforgiveness, you better pick the road to healing and wholeness and forgive because God has forgiven our self-righteous, so innocent and perfect selves.

Scripture Reference:

Matthew 18: 23-35
Nehemiah 9:17

Reflections

1. What health ailments do you currently have?

_____

_____

_____

_____

_____

_____

_____

2. Consider the statistics that point to unforgiveness as a factor in society's biggest killer diseases. How does that make you feel? Journal your thoughts.

_____

_____

_____

_____

_____

_____

_____

3. Pray and ask for forgiveness for any oughts and pain from childhood on that may have contributed to your current health ailments. Write your thoughts.

_____

_____

_____

_____

_____

_____

_____

_____

_____

_____

_____

_____

_____

_____

_____

_____

_____

Day 27

And above all things have fervent
charity among yourselves: for charity
shall cover the multitude of sins.

---

1 Peter 4:8

Checking Our Account

In the banking world, there has to be
enough deposits to cover withdrawals. If
there are more withdrawals than there are
deposits, our account shows insufficient
funds.

Our spiritual bank works much in the
same way. We must make frequent deposits
of prayer and love because life and people
make frequent withdrawals. Love covers
what we can't. When love is not exemplified
and deposited into us, withdrawals from
those we love can bankrupt us. When we
become empty, we end up resentful and over
time unforgiving. Love covers sins and the
shortcomings of others, just like God covers
us. If love didn't cover us, would people
want to be around us?

Vandra Noel

Scripture Reference:

1 Peter 4:7-10
Luke 6: 31-36

Reflections

1. Describe the status of your spiritual account. What is it filled with?

_____

_____

_____

_____

_____

2. Who consistently withdraws from your spiritual bank?

_____

_____

_____

_____

_____

3. How do you respond to people who do not deposit love back into you?

_____

_____

_____

_____

Day 28

Wherefore, my beloved brethren, let every man
be swift to hear, slow to speak, slow to wrath:

For the wrath of man worketh not the
righteousness of God.

James 1: 19-20

Misunderstandings

People can misconstrue something
because they didn't listen with their ears and
instead chose to speak from their fears.
Speaking quickly and out of turn without
fully listening often causes unnecessary
strife. Misunderstandings deposit seeds of
unforgiveness that should've never taken
root in the first place. Learn to just listen first
and have a simple, calm conversation.

Scripture Reference:

Colossians 3:15
Proverbs 15:18

Reflections

1. Has something really simple turned into something big just because someone refused to listen before reacting? Journal your experience.

_____

_____

_____

_____

_____

_____

_____

_____

2. Pray and ask for forgiveness and reconciliation.

_____

_____

_____

_____

_____

Day 29

To everything there is a season, and a time to
every purpose under the heaven:

Ecclesiastes 3:1

Time for Change

Things should never stay the same in our
life. There is a time to cry and to laugh, to
hurt and be happy. There is a time to live and
die, and certainly a time to forgive after
living in unforgiveness.

Change can be hard when we're put in a
bad place emotionally, mentally and
sometimes even physically. However,
forgiveness is exactly the change needed to
undo the toll and control that unforgiveness
had over our lives.

Doing the same thing over and over
again, expecting a different outcome is called
insanity. Change your approach to how you
move, so that your life can improve. Forgive
and allow God to help you see things
differently and in a new way. Let God
upgrade your life!

Scripture Reference:

Joshua 1:9
Deuteronomy 31:8
Proverbs 3:5-6

Reflections

1. Are you suffering in your life or making the necessary steps towards improving it?

_____

_____

_____

_____

2. What areas in your life need improvement?

_____

_____

_____

_____

3. Ask for forgiveness for remaining stagnant in these areas and ask God for guidance and improvement. Journal your thoughts.

_____

_____

_____

_____

Day 30

Then said Jesus, Father, forgive them; for
they know not what they do. And they
parted his raiment, and cast lots.

Luke 23:34

Our Cross Experience

As Jesus was hanging on the cross
willing to die so that you and I could live, He
brought to light the crucial need to forgive.
He said,

*"Father forgive them for they know not what
they do."*

This statement made at the edge of death
was to bring forgiveness to fruition for all of
us. Can we do the same thing in the midst of
our greatest pain and struggle? Can we carry
our Cross and plead on behalf of those
who've hurt us,

*"Father Forgive them for they know not what
they've done."*

Thank God that Jesus already paid the
price. So why are we trying to pay for
something we can't afford? Don't allow your

cross experience to be in vain by holding on to unforgiveness. They may have crucified your character, your hope, and stripped you of everything you had. However, when you forgive them, I promise God will bury all the hurt and resurrect you so you'll be free and stronger than you have ever been before! Believe me, I'm a witness.

Scripture Reference:

Matthew 5:44
Acts 7:60

Reflections

1. What experiences in your life do you find hard to forgive?

_____

_____

_____

_____

_____

_____

_____

2. Imagine yourself taking the place of Jesus. Knowing your death will save the kingdom, would you still do it? Journal your thoughts.

_____

_____

_____

_____

_____

_____

_____

Don't let your cross experience be in vain!

Final Moments of Clarity...

Redeeming the time, because the days are
evil. Wherefore be ye not unwise, but
understanding what the will of the Lord is.

Ephesians 5:16-17

No Time to Play!

Live your best life. Don't waste time with
the devil and his minions. Let go of the
foolishness that has you bound in
unforgiveness. None of us know the day nor
the hour when we will die, so why waste
another second of your life being mad at
someone else?

God's will is for us to forgive, be free,
and live our life abundantly! Smile and live
like today is your last. Let your first step to
freedom be forgiveness! Now that you've
made the first step to forgive walk in your
best life!

Scripture Reference:

Colossians 4:5
Galatians 1:4

Reflections

1. Journal your thoughts. What does your best life look like?

_____

_____

_____

_____

_____

_____

_____

_____

_____

_____

_____

_____

_____

_____

_____

_____

_____

2. You have unpacked and unloaded unforgiveness through these 30 days. What final remnants of hindrances do you believe you still have? Pray to God to release it.

_____

_____

_____

_____

_____

_____

_____

_____

_____

_____

_____

_____

_____

_____

_____

_____

_____

Faith Walk Assignments

Balloon Release

Get 3 balloons in the color of your preference and a black marker. On the first balloon, use the black marker to write the feelings you need to release. On the second balloon, write the offense or offenses. Lastly, write the names of the people or persons you need to forgive on the third balloon. Say this prayer as you release the balloons.

Heavenly Father,

I come to you broken and ready to be free from the bondage of unforgiveness. I'm doing this balloon release by faith for the Father, Son and the Holy Ghost. When I release these balloons in the air, I am releasing my will to handle it, control it, fix it, and change it. God, only you can change it, but only I can release it to you for the change. Now I walk in freedom from this day forward in Jesus name.

Amen

Camp Fire

Write the things that you have not forgiven
yourself and others for on a piece of paper.
When you are finished, fold it and say this
prayer:

Heavenly Father,

*I come by faith releasing everything and everyone
that has created a road block in my life. By faith, I
take this out of my hands and place it in the fire to
burn and never return. I believe I will have
beauty for my ashes! I will not look back, but I
will move forward. I'm looking to you for ordered
steps and a healed heart. I'm releasing this now in
Jesus name.*

Amen

Mirror, Mirror

Many times we can't face the person in the mirror to forgive them. That's why we run nonstop, cover up, and hide behind a mask that lies daily instead of healing. Look in the mirror and tell yourself the following:

YOU ARE SPECIAL!
YOU ARE BEAUTIFUL!
YOU ARE ENOUGH!
YOU ARE NOT YOUR MISTAKE!
YOU ARE NOT WHAT PEOPLE SAY!
YOU ARE A CONQUEROR!
YOU WERE BUILT FOR IT!

Hold yourself tight like no has and say,

I LOVE YOU, I FORGIVE YOU and I NEED YOU TO SURVIVE.

Vandra Noel

Other Books By This Author

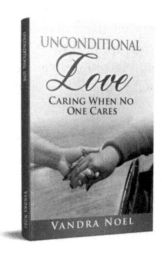

Get connected with
Author Vandra Noel on social media

 Vandra Noel

 Mrs. V. Noel

30 Days of Forgiveness